Alfred's Basic Piano Library
Piano
Duet Book · Level 3

CONTENTS

FOREWORD

While this book of duets is correlated with the corresponding level of Alfred's Basic Piano Library, teachers should be aware that the pieces are written in a manner which makes them highly adaptable to almost any other method. The secondo parts, which can be played by the teacher, parent, or a more advanced student, are delightful accompaniments which serve to enhance the student's part. The primo is "complete" in itself, thus creating little solos which become even more fun when performed as a duet! It is hoped that these duets will bring a smile to the faces of teachers, students, and audiences whether they are performed at the lesson, at home, or on the recital hall stage.

Dennis Alexander

DUET PART (Student plays 1 octave higher)

PENGUIN PARADE

Use after ON TOP OF OLD SMOKY, LESSON BOOK 3 (page 4).

PENGUIN PARADE

DUET PART (Student plays 1 octave higher)

JUGGLING CLOWNS

Use after ALPINE MELODY (page 8).

JUGGLING CLOWNS

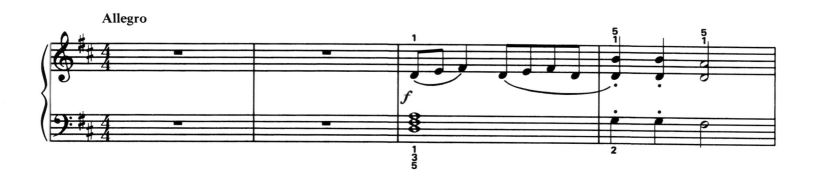

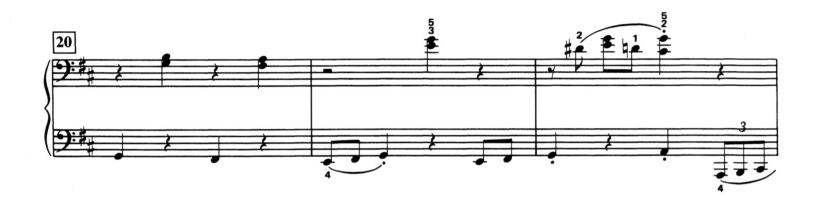

DUET PART (Student plays 1 octave higher)

SWINGIN' ALONG

Use after LIGHT & BLUE (page 12).

SWINGIN' ALONG*

*The pairs of eighth notes may be played
a bit unevenly, in a "lilting" style:

long   short, long   short, etc.

DUET PART (Student plays 1 octave higher)

HYMN PRELUDE

Use after ROMAN HOLIDAY (page 14).

HYMN PRELUDE

Andante moderato

DUET PART (Student plays 1 octave higher)

BUBBLEGUM RAG

Use after CASEY JONES (page 21).

BUBBLEGUM RAG

DUET PART (Student plays 1 octave higher)

ECHO WALTZ

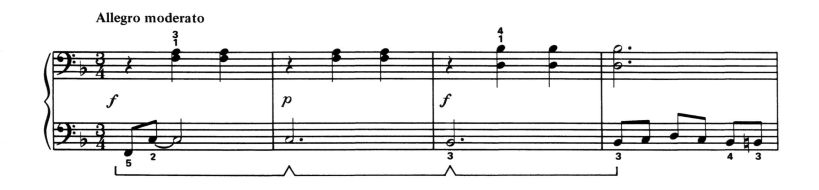

Use after A DAY IN VIENNA (page 22).

ECHO WALTZ

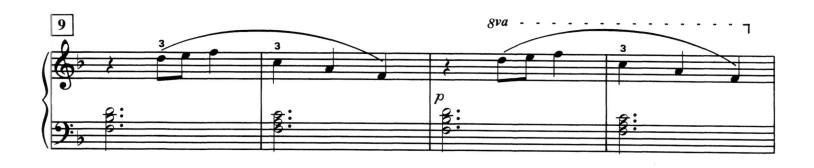

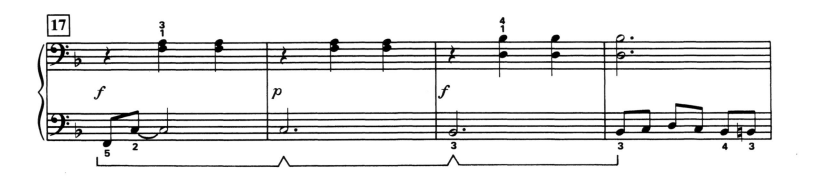

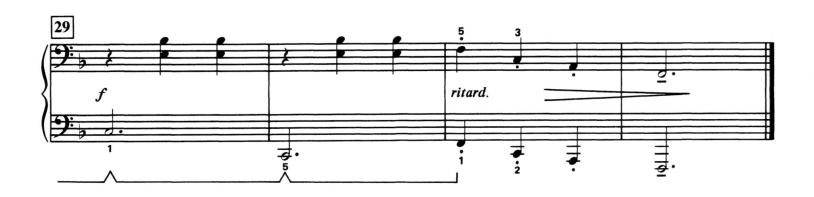

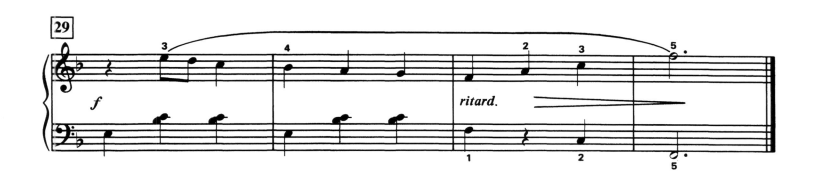

DUET PART (Student plays 1 octave higher)

MUFFIN MAN VARIATIONS

Use after THE MAJOR & THE MINOR (page 28.)

MUFFIN MAN VARIATIONS

Allegro

KEY OF A MINOR
(relative of C MAJOR)

KEY OF F MAJOR
Key Signature: 1 flat (B♭)

KEY OF C MAJOR
Key Signature: no #, no ♭.

DUET PART (Student plays 1 octave higher)

SPANISH INTERMEZZO

Andante moderato

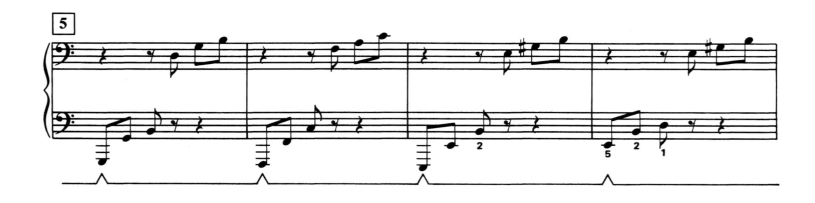

Use after FANDANGO (page 32).

SPANISH INTERMEZZO

Andante moderato

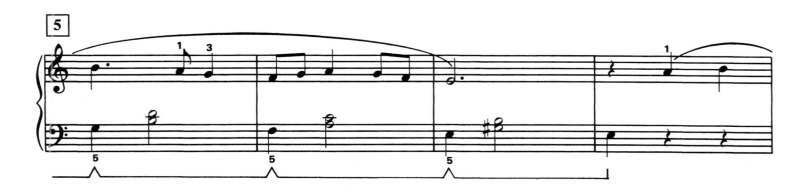

*Secondo pedals if played as a duet.

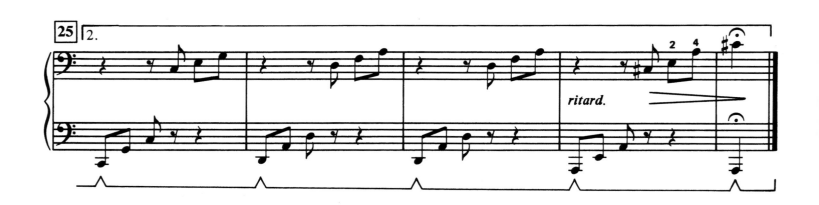

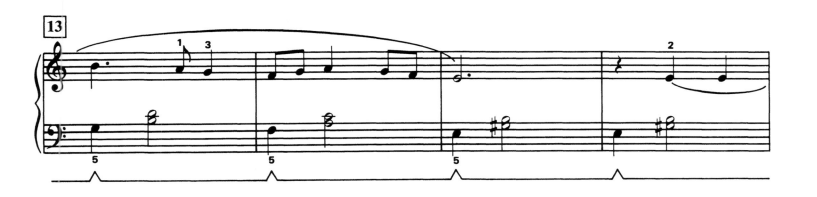

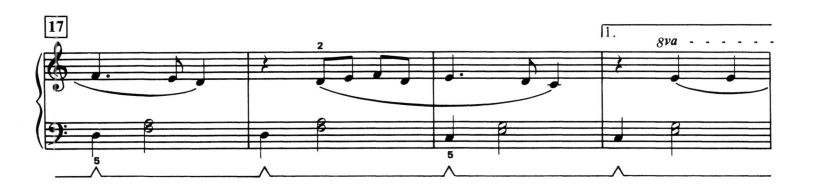

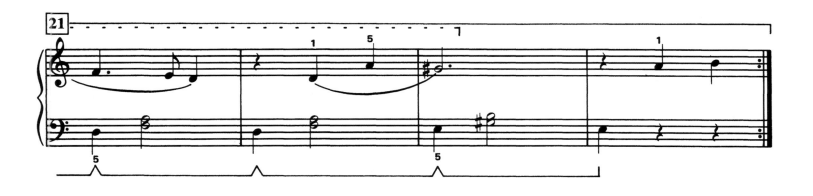

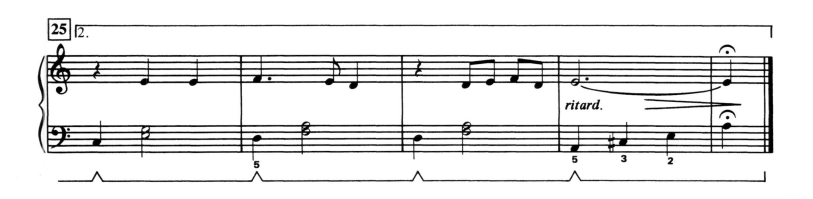

DUET PART (Student plays 1 octave higher)

HANG GLIDERS

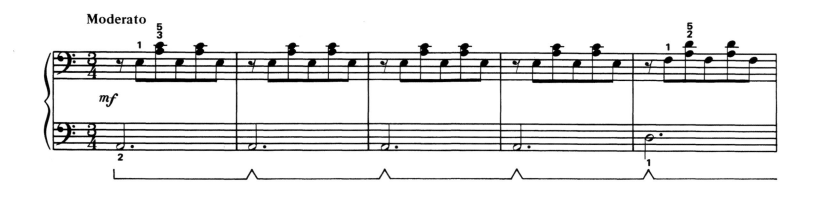

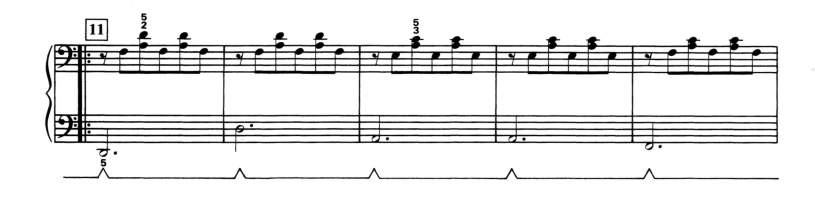

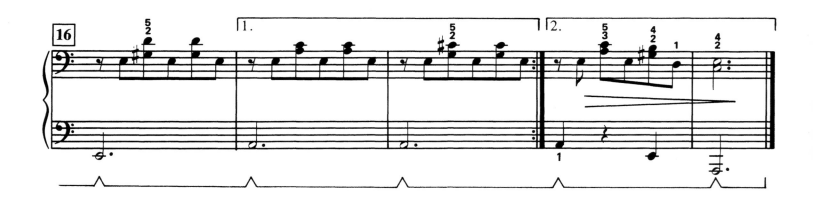

Use after INTERMEZZO (page 36).

HANG GLIDERS

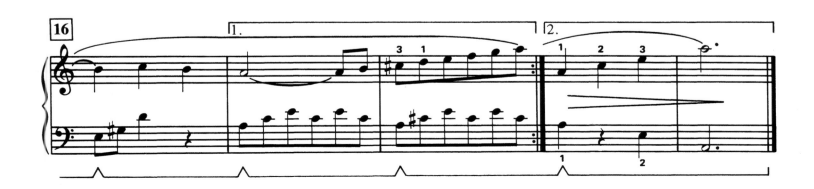

28

DUET PART (Student plays 1 octave higher)

SONATINA IN F

Use after RAISINS & ALMONDS (page 40).

SONATINA IN F

DUET PART (Student plays 1 octave higher)

TARANTELLA

Use after LA RASPA (page 44).

TARANTELLA

32